This journal belongs to

....

Date

....

The future
is as bright
as the promises
of God.

WILLIAM CAREY

We think God's love rises and falls with our performance.
It doesn't.... He loves you for whose you are: you are His child.
MAX LUCADO

The LORD *your God is with you, the Mighty Warrior who saves.*
He will take great delight in you; in his love he will no longer rebuke you,
but will rejoice over you with singing.
ZEPHANIAH 3:17 NIV

*G*od's own skillful hands knit you together, His watchful eyes gazed on you....
Long before technology ordered the first sonogram, God watched you
suck your thumb in your mother's womb. Amazing, isn't it?
BETH MOORE

The LORD directs the steps of the godly. He delights in every detail of their lives. Though they stumble, they will never fall, for the LORD holds them by the hand.
PSALM 37:23-24 NLT

We do not understand the intricate pattern of the stars in their courses, but we know that He who created them does, and that just as surely as He guides them, He is charting a safe course for us.

BILLY GRAHAM

*I'll take the hand of those who don't know the way,
who can't see where they're going. I'll be a personal guide to them,
directing them through unknown country.*
ISAIAH 42:16 MSG

*L*ift up your eyes. Your heavenly Father waits to bless you—
in inconceivable ways to make your life
what you never dreamed it could be.
ANNE ORTLUND

In the proper season I will send the showers they need. There will be showers of blessing.
EZEKIEL 34:26 NLT

I will let God's peace infuse every part of today. As the chaos swirls and life's demands pull at me on all sides, I will breathe in God's peace that surpasses all understanding.

ANNIE FLINT

Don't worry about anything; instead, pray about everything.
Tell God what you need, and thank him for all he has done. Then you will
experience God's peace, which exceeds anything we can understand.
PHILIPPIANS 4:6-7 NLT

*Y*ou are a child of your heavenly Father. Confide in Him.
Your faith in His love and power can never be bold enough.
BASILEA SCHLINK

For everyone who asks receives; the one who seeks finds;
and to the one who knocks, the door will be opened.
MATTHEW 7:8 NIV

Where are you? Start there. Openly and freely declare your need to the One who cares deeply.
CHARLES R. SWINDOLL

....

....

....

....

....

....

....

....

....

....

....

....

....

....

....

....

....

....

....

....

....

*Trust in him at all times, you people; pour out your hearts
to him, for God is our refuge.*
PSALM 62:8 NIV

We must take our troubles to the Lord, but we must do
more than that; we must leave them there.
HANNAH WHITALL SMITH

Give your burdens to the LORD, and he will take care of you.
PSALM 55:22 NLT

You pay God a compliment by asking great things of Him.
TERESA OF AVILA

I tell you, whatever you ask in prayer,
believe that you have received it, and it will be yours.
MARK 11:24 ESV

*L*et the first act when waking be to place yourself, your heart,
mind, faculties, your whole being, in God's hands.
Ask Him to take entire possession of you, to be the guide of your soul,
your life, your wisdom, your strength.

H. L. SIDNEY LEAR

I am always with you; you hold me by my right hand.
PSALM 73:23 NIV

God hears and answers.... His ear is ever open to the cry of His children.

E. M. BOUNDS

I love those who love me; and those who diligently seek me will find me.
Riches and honor are with me, enduring wealth and righteousness.
PROVERBS 8:17–18 NASB

God has designs on our future...and He has designed us for the future.
He has given us something to do in the future that no one else can do.
RUTH SENTER

*All the days ordained for me were written in your book
before one of them came to be.*
PSALM 139:16 NIV

One single grateful thought raised to heaven is the most perfect prayer.
G. E. LESSING

How abundant are the good things that you have stored up for those who fear you,
that you bestow in the sight of all, on those who take refuge in you.
PSALM 31:19 NIV

No matter where we are, God can hear us from there!

How gracious [the Lord] will be when you cry for help!
As soon as he hears, he will answer you.
ISAIAH 30:19 NIV

*Trust the past to the mercy of God, the present to His love,
and the future to His Providence.*
ST. AUGUSTINE

Keep on asking, and you will receive what you ask for. Keep on seeking, and you will find. Keep on knocking, and the door will be opened to you.
LUKE 11:9 NLT

God's heart is the most sensitive and tender of all.
No act goes unnoticed, no matter how insignificant or small.
RICHARD J. FOSTER

In Christ we can come before God with freedom and without fear.
We can do this through faith in Christ.
EPHESIANS 3:12 NCV

*O*ur inner happiness depends not on what we experience but on the degree of our gratitude to God, whatever the experience.
ALBERT SCHWEITZER

The LORD *is my strength and shield. I trust him with all my heart.*
He helps me, and my heart is filled with joy. I burst out in songs of thanksgiving.
PSALM 28:7 NLT

Do not be afraid to enter the cloud that is settling down on your life.
God is in it. The other side is radiant with His glory.

L. B. COWMAN

When you pass through the waters, I will be with you;
and when you pass through the rivers, they will not sweep over you.
ISAIAH 43:2 NIV

We shall steer safely through every storm, so long as our heart is right, our intention fervent, our courage steadfast, and our trust fixed on God.

ST. FRANCIS DE SALES

The Lord *grants wisdom! From his mouth come knowledge and understanding…*
He is a shield to those who walk with integrity.
He…protects those who are faithful to him.
PROVERBS 2:6-8 NLT

*B*ring your soul to the Great Physician—exactly as you are, even and especially at your worst moment.... For it is in such moments that you will most readily sense His healing presence.

TERESA OF AVILA

May your unfailing love come to me, LORD,
your salvation according to your promise.
PSALM 119:41 NIV

God's friendship is the unexpected joy we find
when we reach His outstretched hand.
JANET L. SMITH

You make known to me the path of life; you will fill me with joy
in your presence, with eternal pleasures at your right hand.
PSALM 16:11 NIV

God wants to continually add to us, to develop and enlarge us—
always building on what He has already taught and built in us.
Never be afraid to trust an unknown future to a known God.

CORRIE TEN BOOM

I cry out to God Most High,
to God who will fulfill his purpose for me.
PSALM 57:2 NLT

When I give thanks for the seemingly microscopic,
I make a place for God to grow within me. This, this makes me full.
ANN VOSKAMP

It is good to give thanks to the LORD and to sing praises to Your name, O Most High; to declare Your lovingkindness in the morning and Your faithfulness by night.
PSALM 92:1-2 NASB

Therefore will I trust You [LORD God] always, though I may seem to be lost
and in the shadow of death. I will not fear, for You are ever with me.
And You will never leave me to face my perils alone.
THOMAS MERTON

Fear not, for I am with you; be not dismayed, for I am your God.
I will strengthen you, yes, I will help you,
I will uphold you with My righteous right hand.
ISAIAH 41:10 NKJV

That is God's call to us—simply to be people who are content
to live close to Him and to renew the kind of life in which
the closeness is felt and experienced.

THOMAS MERTON

I have learned to be content in whatever circumstances I am.
I know how to get along with humble means,
and I also know how to live in prosperity.
PHILIPPIANS 4:11-12 NASB

If you have a special need today, focus your full attention on the goodness
and greatness of your Father rather than on the size of your need.
Your need is so small compared to His ability to meet it.

May you have the power to understand, as all God's people should,
how wide, how long, how high, and how deep his love is.
EPHESIANS 3:18 NLT

God created the universe, but He also created you. God knows you, God loves you, and God cares about the tiniest details of your life.

BRUCE BICKEL AND STAN JANTZ

O LORD, you have examined my heart and know everything about me....
You go before me and follow me. You place your hand of blessing on my head.
PSALM 139:1, 5 NLT

God is keenly aware that we are dependent upon Him for life's necessities.
BILLY GRAHAM

Give all your worries to him; because he cares about you.
1 PETER 5:7 NCV

There are only two ways to live your life. One is as though nothing is a miracle. The other is as though everything is a miracle.

RICHARD CRASHAW

If God is for us, who is against us? He who did not spare His own Son,
but delivered Him over for us all,
how will He not also with Him freely give us all things?
ROMANS 8:31-32 NASB

God is always present in the temple of your heart...His home.
And when you come in to meet Him there, you find that it is
the one place of deep satisfaction where every longing is met.

OSWALD CHAMBERS

How lovely are Your dwelling places, O LORD of hosts!
My soul longed and even yearned for the courts of the LORD;
my heart and my flesh sing for joy to the living God.
PSALM 84:1-2 NASB

We need never shout across the spaces to an absent God.
He is nearer than our own soul, closer than our most secret thoughts.
A. W. TOZER

You will keep in perfect peace those whose minds are steadfast,
because they trust in you.
ISAIAH 26:3 NIV

God is always there. Always. Sometimes we lose sight of Him because we take our eyes away. But He is there.

The LORD is good. His unfailing love continues forever,
and his faithfulness continues to each generation.
PSALM 100:5 NLT

*Whatever He may demand of us, He will give us at the moment
the strength and courage that we need.*
FRANÇOIS FÉNELON

Be strong and courageous! Do not be afraid and do not panic before them. For the LORD your God will personally go ahead of you. He will neither fail you nor abandon you.
DEUTERONOMY 31:6 NLT

What higher, more exalted, and more compelling goal
can there be than to know God?

J. I. PACKER

One thing I ask from the Lord, this only do I seek:
that I may dwell in the house of the Lord all the days of my life.
PSALM 27:4 NIV

Everything in life is most fundamentally a gift. And you receive it best, and you live it best, by holding it with very open hands.

LEO O'DONOVAN

I will give you treasures hidden in the darkness—secret riches.
I will do this so you may know that I am the LORD...
the one who calls you by name.
ISAIAH 45:3 NLT

Great faith isn't the ability to believe long and far into the misty future.
It's simply taking God at His word and taking the next step.
JONI EARECKSON TADA

*Blessed are those who trust in the LORD
and have made the LORD their hope and confidence.*
JEREMIAH 17:7 NLT

*L*ord, help me do great things as though they were little,
since I do them with Your powers; and help me to do little things
as though they were great, because I do them in Your Name.
BLAISE PASCAL

Greater is He who is in you than he who is in the world.
1 JOHN 4:4 NASB

There will always be the unknown. There will always be the unprovable.
But faith confronts those frontiers with a thrilling leap.
Then life becomes vibrant with adventure!
ROBERT SCHULLER

With God all things are possible.
MARK 10:27 NKJV

When we call on God, He bends down His ear to listen,
as a father bends down to listen to his little child.
ELIZABETH CHARLES

Examine and see how good the LORD is. Happy is the person who trusts him.
You who belong to the LORD, fear him!
Those who fear him will have everything they need.
PSALM 34:8-9 NCV

$\mathcal{G}$od wants us to approach life, full of expectancy that God is going to be at work in every situation as we grow in our faith in Him.

COLIN URQUHART

*We know that in everything God works
for the good of those who love him.*
ROMANS 8:28 NCV

We must drink deeply from the very Source the deep calm and peace of interior quietude and refreshment of God, allowing the pure water of divine grace to flow plentifully and unceasingly from the Source itself.

MOTHER TERESA

*Whoever drinks of the water that I will give him shall never thirst;
but the water that I will give him will become in him
a well of water springing up to eternal life.*
JOHN 4:13-14 NASB

Remember you are very special to God as His precious child.
He has promised to complete the good work He has begun in you.
As you continue to grow in Him, He will make you a blessing to others.

See what great love the Father has lavished on us,
that we should be called children of God! And that is what we are!
1 JOHN 3:1 NIV

You can talk to God because God listens.
Your voice matters in heaven. He takes you very seriously.
MAX LUCADO

I love the LORD because he hears my voice and my prayer for mercy.
Because he bends down to listen, I will pray as long as I have breath!
PSALM 116:1-2 NLT

The world is full of noise. Might we not set ourselves
to learn silence, stillness, solitude?
ELISABETH ELLIOT

In quietness and confidence is your strength.
ISAIAH 30:15 NLT

God listens in compassion and love, just like we do when our children come to us. He delights in our presence.

RICHARD J. FOSTER

This is the confidence we have in approaching God:
that if we ask anything according to his will, he hears us.
1 JOHN 5:14 NIV

We come this morning—like empty pitchers to a full fountain,
with no merits of our own, O Lord—
open up a window of heaven...and listen this morning.
JAMES WELDON JOHNSON

If you remain in me and follow my teachings,
you can ask anything you want, and it will be given to you.
JOHN 15:7 NCV

Dear Lord...shine through me, and be so in me that every soul I come in contact
with may feel Your presence in my soul.... Let me thus praise You
in the way You love best, by shining on those around me.
JOHN HENRY NEWMAN

I pray that from his glorious, unlimited resources he will empower you with inner strength through his Spirit. Then Christ will make his home in your hearts as you trust in him. Your roots will grow down into God's love and keep you strong.

EPHESIANS 3:16-17 NLT

The Creator thinks enough of you to have sent Someone
very special so that you might have life—
abundantly, joyfully, completely, and victoriously.

I came that they may have life and have it abundantly.
JOHN 10:10 ESV

*J*esus Christ has brought every need, every joy, every gratitude,
every hope of ours before God. He accompanies us
and brings us into the presence of God.
DIETRICH BONHOEFFER

I am convinced that nothing can ever separate us from God's love. Neither death nor life, neither angels nor demons, neither our fears for today nor our worries about tomorrow— not even the powers of hell can separate us from God's love.

ROMANS 8:38 NLT

God wants nothing from us except our needs, and these furnish Him
with room to display His bounty when He supplies them freely....
Not what I have, but what I do not have,
is the first point of contact between my soul and God.
CHARLES H. SPURGEON

My God of mercy shall come to meet me.
PSALM 59:10 NKJV

The "air" which our souls need also envelops all of us at all times
and on all sides. God is round about us...on every hand,
with many-sided and all-sufficient grace.

OLE HALLESBY

*Let us come boldly to the throne of our gracious God.
There we will receive his mercy, and we will find grace
to help us when we need it most.*
HEBREWS 4:16 NLT

*G*ratitude consists in a watchful, minute attention to the particulars of our state,
and to the multitude of God's gifts, taken one by one.
It fills us with a consciousness that God loves and cares for us.
HENRY EDWARD MANNING

The LORD will work out his plans for my life—
for your faithful love, O LORD, endures forever.
PSALM 138:8 NLT

There is no need to plead that the love of God shall fill our hearts as though He were unwilling to fill us.... Love is pressing around us on all sides like air. Cease to resist it and instantly love takes possession.

AMY CARMICHAEL

*Are not five sparrows sold for two pennies? Yet not one of them is forgotten by God.
Indeed, the very hairs of your head are all numbered.
Don't be afraid; you are worth more than many sparrows.*
LUKE 12:6-7 NIV

Allow your dreams a place in your prayers and plans.
God-given dreams can help you move
into the future He is preparing for you.
BARBARA JOHNSON

I know the plans I have for you, declares the L{\scriptsize ORD},
plans for welfare and not for evil, to give you a future and a hope.
JEREMIAH 29:11 ESV

God shall be my hope, my stay, my guide and lantern to my feet.
WILLIAM SHAKESPEARE

He is our God forever and ever, and he will guide us until we die.
PSALM 48:14 NLT

The goodness of God is infinitely more wonderful
than we will ever be able to comprehend.
A. W. TOZER

God can do anything, you know—far more than you could ever imagine or guess or request in your wildest dreams!
EPHESIANS 3:20 MSG

*P*rayer is God's plan to supply man's great and continuous need
with God's great and continuous abundance.

E. M. BOUNDS

The Lord is good to all; he has compassion on all he has made.
All your works praise you, Lord.
PSALM 145:9–10 NIV

My prayers don't change God. But, I am convinced prayer changes me.
Praying boldly boots me out of that stale place of religious habit
into authentic connection with God Himself.
LYSA TERKEURST

My cup brims with blessing. Your beauty and love chase after me every day of my life.
PSALM 23:5-6 MSG

*Prayer is simply talking to God like a friend
and should be the easiest thing we do each day.*
JOYCE MEYER

I no longer call you servants, because a servant does not know
what his master is doing. But I call you friends, because
I have made known to you everything I heard from my Father.
JOHN 15:15 NCV

True prayer is neither a mere mental exercise nor a vocal performance.
It is far deeper than that—it is spiritual transaction
with the Creator of Heaven and Earth.
CHARLES H. SPURGEON

Seek first his kingdom and his righteousness, and all these things will be given to you as well.
MATTHEW 6:33 NIV

*P*rayer is not asking. Prayer is putting oneself in the hands of God, at His disposition, and listening to His voice in the depth of our hearts.
MOTHER TERESA

Those who know your name put their trust in you, for you,
O LORD, have not forsaken those who seek you.
PSALM 9:10 ESV

Any concern too small to be turned into a prayer
is too small to be made into a burden.
CORRIE TEN BOOM

He only is my rock and my salvation;
He is my defense; I shall not be moved.
PSALM 62:6 NKJV

No matter what challenges we face, we can be strengthened with God's power.
We don't have to do it all in our own strength.
ERIN DAVIS

Then Jesus said, "Let's go off by ourselves to a quiet place and rest awhile."
He said this because there were so many people coming and going that Jesus
and his apostles didn't even have time to eat.

MARK 6:31 NLT

If you are at a place in your life where you feel like you can't take one step without the Lord's help, be glad. He has you where He wants you.

STORMIE OMARTIAN

The LORD will fight for you; you need only to be still.
EXODUS 14:14 NIV

We walk without fear, full of hope and courage and strength to do His will,
waiting for the endless good which He is always giving
as fast as He can get us able to take it in.
GEORGE MACDONALD

Have I not commanded you? Be strong and courageous.
Do not be frightened, and do not be dismayed,
for the LORD your God is with you wherever you go.
JOSHUA 1:9 ESV

If God be our God, He will give us peace in trouble. When there is a storm without, He will make peace within. The world can create trouble in peace, but God can create peace in trouble.

THOMAS WATSON

God is our refuge and strength, an ever-present help in trouble.
Therefore we will not fear.
PSALM 46:1-2 NIV

Deep within the center of the soul is a chamber of peace where God lives
and where, if we will enter it and quiet all the other sounds,
we can hear His "gentle whisper."

L. B. COWMAN

Abide in Me, and I in you. As the branch cannot bear fruit of itself, unless it abides in the vine, neither can you, unless you abide in Me.
JOHN 15:4 NKJV

If I could hear Christ praying for me in the next room,
I would not fear a million enemies.
ROBERT MURRAY MCCHEYNE

When I am afraid, I will put my trust in you.
PSALM 56:3 NLT

His strength is perfect when our strength is gone.
He'll carry us when we can't carry on. Raised in His power
the weak become strong. His strength is perfect.
JERRY SALLEY AND STEVEN CURTIS CHAPMAN

"My grace is sufficient for you, for My strength is made perfect in weakness."
Therefore most gladly I will rather boast in my infirmities,
that the power of Christ may rest upon me.
2 CORINTHIANS 12:9 NKJV

No circumstance is so big that He cannot control it.
JERRY BRIDGES

He brought me forth also into a large place;
he delivered me, because he delighted in me.
PSALM 18:19 KJV

God has not promised sun without rain, joy without sorrow, peace without pain.
But God has promised strength for the day, rest for the labor, light for the way,
grace for the trials, help from above, unfailing sympathy, undying love.
ANNIE JOHNSON FLINT

It is God who arms me with strength and keeps my way secure.
He makes my feet like the feet of a deer; he causes me to stand on the heights.
PSALM 18:32-33 NIV

Joy is the settled assurance that God is in control of all the details of my life,
the quiet confidence that ultimately everything is going to be all right,
and the determined choice to praise God in all things.

KAY WARREN

The eyes of the LORD range throughout the earth to strengthen those whose hearts are fully committed to him.
2 CHRONICLES 16:9 NIV

*B*efore me, even as behind, God is, and all is well.

JOHN GREENLEAF WHITTIER

God has said, "Never will I leave you; never will I forsake you."
So we say with confidence, "The Lord is my helper; I will not be afraid.
What can mere mortals do to me?"
HEBREWS 13:5-6 NIV

*P*rayer, when we are faithful to it and practice it at regular times, slowly leads us to an experience of rest and opens us to God's active presence.
HENRI NOUWEN

Draw near to God and He will draw near to you.
JAMES 4:8 NKJV

If you look at the world, you'll be distressed. If you look within, you'll be depressed. But if you look at Christ, you'll be at rest.

CORRIE TEN BOOM

....

....

....

....

....

....

....

....

....

....

....

....

....

....

....

....

....

....

....

....

....

The LORD God is our sun and our shield. He gives us grace and glory.
The LORD will withhold no good thing from those who do what is right.
O LORD of Heaven's Armies, what joy for those who trust in you.
PSALM 84:11-12 NLT

*S*peak, move, act in peace, as if you were in prayer.
In truth, this is prayer.
FRANÇOIS FÉNELON

Don't let your hearts be troubled.
Trust in God, and trust also in me.
JOHN 14:1 NLT

All that is good, all that is true, all that is beautiful, all that is beneficent,
be it great or small, be it perfect or fragmentary, natural as well as
supernatural, moral as well as material, comes from God.
JOHN HENRY NEWMAN

The LORD *gives his people strength. The* LORD *blesses them with peace.*
PSALM 29:11 NLT

God speaks in the silence of the heart. Listening is the beginning of prayer.
MOTHER TERESA

Be still before the LORD and wait patiently for him.
PSALM 37:7 NIV

Ellie Claire
Hachette Book Group
1290 Avenue of the Americas, New York, NY 10104
ellieclaire.com

First Edition: August 2019
Ellie Claire is a division of Hachette Book Group, Inc. The Ellie Claire name
and logo are trademarks of Hachette Book Group, Inc.

The publisher is not responsible for websites (or their content) that are not
owned by the publisher.

Print book interior by Bart Dawson. Compiled by Jill Jones.

ISBN 9781633262164 (hardcover)

Printed in China

RRD-C

10 9 8 7 6 5 4 3 2 1